CW01507049

Sleep

Paralysis

How to identify and combat the entities
that attack you when you're most vulnerable

JOHNNY FIVE

Cover and Layout Design: Creativindie

Table of Contents

Chapter 1

Introduction

What is sleep paralysis? Sleep paralysis is a state during waking up or falling asleep in which a person is aware but unable to move or speak. When you start to slumber, there is a transition that takes place when you initially fall asleep. This transition is known as REM sleep, or rapid eye movement. During this phase our physical brains are most active and dreams are most intense or vivid. Right before the REM state occurs, the brain releases two chemicals to prevent the body from acting out what is happening in the dream state, basically paralysis. These two neurotransmitters are called gamma-aminobutyric acid, or GABA, and glycine.

When we sleep, we fade from our physical body and our astral body leaves. Our astral body is our second body or spirit body. When we are born we have an umbilical cord attached to our physical body and our astral body has a silver cord attached to our physical body to keep the astral body and physical body attached and connected. This cord is severed when we die and ascend into the next phase of existence. The state of sleep paralysis occurs when the physical body wakes up before the astral body has returned back to the physical body.

What causes you to wake up could be several factors but one of the factors this book focuses on is the presence of entities. Since they enter into your space energetically, your "spidey senses" will go off and it wakes you up. Since there is no loud bang, loud noise, or something physically touching you for your physical body to react to causing it to wake up, it continues to stay in the paralysis state. It is during this interaction you might be able to see some things that would otherwise be invisible. The physical eyes are open but you are seeing through a portion of the sight of your astral body which will allow you to potentially see other beings inside your room.

Science will tell you that anything you see during sleep paralysis is a hallucination and that your dream is appearing in your surroundings as your deepest fears.

Science would like you to believe that to keep you ignorant. I am here to reveal to you that it is not a hallucination. In this book, I am going to explain the metaphysical reasoning of why this occurs as they are multiple reasons for this phenomenon.

There are multiple possibilities for why sleep paralysis can happen but this book will only focus on one aspect. Sleep paralysis can occur during astral projecting, see my book *Dream Walker* to learn what this is and how to do it, or when an entity visits you to extract some of your energy. I will focus mostly on providing you with information about the entity factor. Factors such as what to look for, how to recognize them, and how to protect yourself against them. This book can be used to guide you through a process of elimination to help figure out the underlying issue. The book will give clarity to those who have been or are currently being affected by sleep paralysis.

My knowledge on this subject does not come from any online source or resources. This experience is entirely based upon the wisdom that I have gained through having dealt with this phenomenon throughout my life since I was a child. The main difference that sets me apart from the majority of people experiencing this is that I had always had the natural sight, or ability, to see the entities as plain as day and they would speak to me. I learned how to communicate back to them when I got much older. I always tried to speak back to tell them to go away during the paralysis state but my mouth was always bound. I would just mumble as it's a natural reflex as a human to communicate with the mouth. They were not concealed as a shadowy figure, nor were they "demons." They have all been humanoid looking types of beings. There are literally thousands of these beings that live in another dimension co-existing among us. I will provide descriptions of the most common ones however most of them are not comparable to anything within our reality.

Growing up, these beings attacked me all the time and I felt powerless to be able to do anything to prevent them from assaulting me. These assaults were not of the physical kind, the pain was more energetic and sometimes lingered after waking so that I felt like I was feeling it physically. Some beings will leave physical marks on you that you can see as faint scratches on your body. As humans, we sustain ourselves by eating food and drinking water. Entities do not need to eat food or drink water to survive, they survive by harvesting energy. So we have 7 major gates that surround our body that rotate in a circle. These 7 gates are known as the 7 major chakras and are seen as an aura surrounding our bodies. These energies are naturally invisible to the human eye however, they are connected to our spine.

We as humans are essentially batteries. We create energy within ourselves consistently and some people such as myself can see this energy surrounding people and animals (see my book _Psychic Sight_ to learn to see auras and understand the 7 major chakras). Entities survive off of extracting this energy from us. They feed off the lower chakra gates related to fear and sexuality. There are entities that prefer to extract the sexual energy from humans so they will come to us in the form of a sexual dream and extract the sexual energy which in turn results as you having an orgasm or "wet dream." If you are unaware you are being consensual, they will play nice and create a sexual dream when they visit to virtually distract you in a way by disguising themselves as someone you would be physically attracted to. When you start to recognize this or what they are doing and try to disallow it they will take it by force which can be related to the claims of people claiming they are being or have been raped during sleep paralysis by a "succubus," or "incubus." This extraction of energy will leave you unusually fatigued in the mornings and not understanding why you could still be exhausted, tired, or worn out, still after 7-8 hours or so of rest. It is because you are being siphoned of energy.

It took me many years to learn how to defend myself against these seemingly impossible to defend against beings. In my teenage years, I went to churches, Christian non-denominational churches. I would have such bad encounters with these beings that I would seek spiritual guidance and advice from pastors at these churches. They were not able to help me just offer some general advice such as praying to God, saying the name of Jesus when they appear, etc.. Which of all none of these techniques worked. The attacks became more consistent as time went on and I started seeking the advice of spiritual individuals outside of the church. Even the spiritual group of individuals I spoke with and contacted could only offer general advice as well which also did not work. I came to terms that my journey involved discovering the answer to the questions I had and then assisting in making the information widely available to those interested.

One of the spiritual persons I had contacted was not able to relate to my experiences but provided some general methods that one, in particular, ended up being the best defense against negative entities. This individual I actually contacted him in regards to another situation involving my cats. Weeks later I brought some of my experiences up in conversation and although he could not relate to my experiences, he talked to me about trying to place a Clear Quartz Crystal in each corner in my room.

I had no real knowledge about crystals at this time and when he told me that I thought it was the silliest thing I had ever heard. Nonetheless, I went to a local metaphysical store and bought some. I left it on my table for several weeks because I did not believe they would work and I was too lazy to move furniture around so that

I could get them placed in each corner. I became desperate after an encounter with a succubus during a sleep paralysis episode. I had never seen anything so terrifying.

She was on top of me, looking straight into my eyes as I laid there paralyzed, unable to move. She was seemingly surprised that I could see her, she started speaking to me and I spoke back through telepathy. The experience was so terrifying that I did not want to remember what she said to me so I did not write it down or give any energy to the thought of remembering. This was a long time ago.

I am more confident around entities nowadays and speak to them with authority and without fear so I remember all my conversations these days with these beings. Anyways, I was afraid to sleep after that encounter because I was so terrified. Desperate, I went ahead and tried setting up the barrier. After setting it up and going to bed that night, I randomly woke up exactly once an hour every hour until I had to get up for work the next morning. This is the moment I saw a significant decrease in the visits from astral entities. So, what are entities?

Chapter 2

What is an Entity?

Is an entity a spirit? Is a spirit an entity? What is the difference? An entity is a living being that exists in another dimension within our reality. There are many dimensions other than the dimension we operate in. These dimensions are not a place you can go to or travel to, you have to phase, or tune into them.

See my book _Dream Walker_ to learn about the different dimensions and the techniques used to visit them. A spirit is a being that is dead or has deceased, some that have not yet passed on into the next phase of existence or are unaware that they are deceased. The main difference between an entity and a spirit is one is living and one is non-living however both existent. Entities exist in the 4th dimension and we exist in the 3rd dimension. There are thousands of different beings that exist in this realm. All of our mythical lore creatures come from the beings that exist in the 4th dimension. Beings such as fairies, dragons, mermaids, centaurs, succubus, incubus, imps, unicorn, griffins, etc..

Like in our own society, you have negative people and you have positive people. Same for the beings in the 4th dimension, you have negative beings and positive beings. This book will mostly focus on the common negative entities one is most likely to encounter on their journey. When one learns to visit the 4th-dimensional realm, they would probably be excited to communicate with any beings they might encounter.

They would quickly learn that just like walking up to a stranger within our own reality, they may not want to talk back or be bothered. One has to be extremely careful when communicating with beings that exist in other realms. You have to develop the ability to discern which are for your highest good and which are trying to deceive and manipulate you. One can accidentally visit these realms while sleeping or on a psychedelic trip. Psychedelics can remove the filter that prevents humans from perceiving the other realms simultaneously so that it does not distract us from our day to day life. Psychedelics can put you in harm's way if you have no understanding of these other realms and the beings that exist in them.

Using psychedelics may inevitably cross your path with a negative entity and once they see or interact with you, they can place an energetic mark/implant on your body so that they can find you again. This is an example of some stories you might have heard online or from a friend who did drugs and then suddenly they started to be haunted by a being or "shadowy figure."

These marks are often holes left in our energetic auric field by entities that are naturally invisible to the human physical eyes although there are some spiritual people out there who can see and repair these holes. Negative entities often only visit at night and while we sleep since we are defenseless at this time. They can teleport to the area by opening a portal to the marked target's area that is sleeping and invade their dream and create illusions inside the dream or influencing the dream. Entities can look upon us and know everything about us. There are no secrets hidden from them about ourselves. Upon looking at us they know our fears, likes, dislikes, fetishes, habits, lusts, desires, secrets, all is revealed to them. You might wonder how that is possible. I have the ability to do the same thing to a smaller degree so with knowing that, it is not improbable at all. I can see the auras of people and animals.

Upon seeing the color of the aura, understanding what the color is linked to, I can tell a great deal of information about a person. I get asked a lot, how did you know that about me? I can tell a person about themselves without having ever met them by seeing the color of their aura and possessing the knowledge of what the color means.

It is not a telepathic knowingness, it is simply an understanding of the energy emitting off of the person. Since I can do this myself, it is no surprise that entities can see further about ourselves than we can ourselves. I believe the aura is the physical blueprint of a person's soul. If the physical blueprint can be seen in the physical, then the blueprint itself can probably be seen outside of the physical by beings that exist outside of it.

Through experience I came to figure out entities

leave you with a business card, so to speak, letting you know they visited. I will call it an energetic signature. When I cleansed and opened my third eye, was more accepting of spirituality and not denying it, I started noticing in these dreams where I was attacked or had sleep paralysis episodes, I could see an animation playing with my eyes opened or closed immediately after waking up.

This animation seemed like a projector following the movements of my eyes and showing exactly what the entity looked like. This plays like an animation movie, seeing a cartoon animation in the physical, playing before your very eyes. I usually saw them dancing, staring back at me just glaring, or moving side to side repeating the same motions as the vision of them dissipates over 20 seconds upon waking as they fade away back into their realm. Our physical eyes are active in the light, or when open. Our third eye is active in darkness, or when eyes are closed. Upon waking you stop seeing with the third eye, which is our sixth sense and allows us to see the metaphysical, and your vision reverts back to the physical. There is this separation filter so that we humans can function on our tasks and experiences in the physical without distraction from the metaphysical. Again, drugs remove this filter so people on certain substances continually see the blend of both realities during the duration of the substance and it can drive them mad or lead them into a psychiatric facility.

Again, we are not supposed to see both realms simultaneously because humans on average would not be able to handle it. It would be different if we grew up as a child to an adult experiencing both realms then we would be accustomed to it. Since we are not, it could cause great fear and prevent the development and growth our soul seeks in the current incarnation. We naturally fear what we do not understand.

Furthermore, the entities never reveal themselves in dreams so you see them disguised as a fear of yours, a physically attractive person, an evil person/character, childhood frightening character, animals with distorted faces, etc.. I started visiting these entities in the astral when I became older, wiser, and of course, learned how to do it and protect myself. I noticed that they matched the way they looked from the faint energetic signature. In person, they were their actual size and they looked similar to an animation type of character or how a CGI character would look.

I will also bring to light that when I learned to leave the body, I noticed there were two small beings always with me, my two cats. Outside of the physical realm, they look like two small fairy-animalistic beings that are similar to what a pomeranian looks like. They look animalistic in nature although they do not look like a cat or dog. One is white and the other is black. They are a negative and positive being, a type of yin and yang duo. Sometimes they show themselves like this, other times they show themselves as they are but with a third eye open between their brows.

In the next chapter, I am going to go over some of the most common entities I encountered along my journey. Keep in mind everyone's experience and personal journey are unique so not everyone will have the same experience and one may not encounter the same common ones I have encountered or any at all.

Chapter 3

Types of Entities

I am going to go over some of the most common entities I have encountered throughout my life. Each entity has its own unique set of characteristics, abilities, traits, etc. As I mentioned in the previous chapter, entities leave you with a signature letting you know that they visited. This is noticed immediately upon waking.

Those with a cleansed and activated pineal gland, see my book *Psychic Sight* to learn how to cleanse and activate the pineal gland (third eye), will see what appears to be an animation playing while your eyes are open or closed of a faint vision of what that entity looks like which disappears over 20 seconds. If you do not have a cleansed pineal gland, you will likely never see these beings, their signatures, or anything outside of this reality. It is very faint to see all of the characteristics but you can make out pretty much what it looks like. Some of them look like familiar things we could see in our reality however most are incomparable to anything physically on Earth. Some look like a humanoid type of beings while others look like an animation of an animalistic being you might see in a movie like *Avatar*.

I have seen tons of different signatures of entities after they have visited me in my sleep to extract my energy. Sometimes these visits would leave me with physical scratch marks on my body or sometimes an incredibly sharp pain somewhere along my spine (where our chakras are located).

I have never necessarily feared these beings for the most part since part of my experience involved interaction with them throughout my life. I hoped to learn from them. With each visit, I would study the common things that they did or noticeable traits. I hoped to obtain this knowledge to teach others about them to prevent them from having to go through the same years of torment I went through. After learning how to astral travel, see my book *Dream Walker* to learn this technique, I decided to visit them for a change and surprise them. So I show up and they are surprised to see me like, the hell are you doing here? We go to you, you do not come to us. Once in their realm, I saw how they matched exactly how their signatures looked. Beings that I cannot begin to figure out how to describe how they looked. The beings in this particular visit looked like a levitating Sonic the Hedgehog and there was a red one that looked like a levitating Knuckles. Obviously they do not look exactly like these characters but it is the closest things I can compare them to.

So in the astral, the power of imagination manifests instantly upon intention. This power exists in the physical reality however since we cannot see it, we do not believe in our imagination. Like air exists, the power of imagination exists, it is only invisible to the human eye naturally as to not cause a distraction or unwanted attention to ourselves. Most of them allowed me to pass by but the blue one zipped right into my face. I became defensive, imagining a circular purple barrier around me. To my surprise, the shield appeared as a protective barrier around me. This is when these beings were instructed to back away and let me pass through. This is when I discovered that these beings were a type of pet or minion. I do not know if they were conjured up but since magic exists in the astral realm, it would not surprise me. I then came face to face with this feminine being that had been energetically bonded with me for some time extracting my energy. She may not have ever shown her true self but she was appearing to me as a human woman.

Through communication with her, I learned that whatever question I asked, she seemed to have to answer, as if it were law in that realm. Although she would answer some of my questions she answered in a way that was sly, concealing some information, or not elaborating. I came to understanding through reading between the lines of her deceitfulness that there is some type of law that beings are not allowed to visit humans. Or at least some humans specifically are not allowed to be tampered with such as visiting them and extracting their energy. I came to understand she was not allowed to visit me herself, so she sent her pets, or minions, to take my energy and bring it back to her. With this understanding, I know that there are beings that send minions on their behalf to do their bidding so that they will not get caught doing it themselves. I had three separate encounters with this being after she taught me how to return to her inside an empty house in the astral. She was not malicious although she was not for my highest good. I mean I get it, beings gotta do what they gotta do to survive.

Are we going to get mad at a lion for hunting down a gazelle to eat in order to survive? So I could understand why she was doing what she was doing to me and I was not upset about it. Now that I consciously knew, was I going to continue to let her take my energy with no barter? I offered her an exchange. I would allow her to extract some of my energy in exchange for her knowledge about the astral realm so that I could teach others about it in the physical realm. The only technique she taught me was how to return to her in the astral. Going forward she would not teach me anything else as she mentioned she was not allowed to. I could see through her deceit so I stopped visiting since our paths only crossed for a lesson to be learned and then to move on. A useful technique no doubt. Nonetheless, it was only taught to me for her personal gain so we could meet in private and she could harvest a small portion of my energy. This technique is to get to specific places in the astral, I explain how to do this technique in my book _Dream Walker_.

In the physical realm, we are governed by time, space, and matter. In order for us to get to point A from point B, we have to move there. Beings in the astral are not governed by time, space, or matter. To get to places, all they have to do is create a portal and they go through it. They have the ability to instantly travel, or instant transmission. They wait for us to fall asleep when we are most vulnerable then they come through a portal. Time does not exist outside of our reality, it is a construct constructed by man. Time is an illusion. Man calculated how many intervals happened in one Earth rotation and called it time and now we allow ourselves to be governed by it.

I will now go over commonly visiting and most recognizable beings, based on my experience, that I have encountered.

Guides

I will start off the list with a group of positive entities.

These beings are not easy to reach or to speak to face to face. These beings are in a realm higher than the realm where negative beings exist. This group of beings exist in the 5th dimension which is a realm where only those who resonate with the love frequency reside. Only positivity and love exists in this realm.

These beings are usually referred to as spiritual guides, angels, spiritual council, etc. These beings help and guide us from behind the scenes. On average, there are 3-4 guides assigned to every soul currently occupying a human body. The higher the dimension, the harder it is to travel to via astral travel. The purer you are internally, the higher your vibration, the more likely you are able to visit the higher dimensions and encounter the beings there. These guides will likely only show themselves to you as a human so I do not know what they actually look like. If you were a child, you would see them as children. As you age, they change how they appear to you for relatability. They directly speak with you daily via "angel numbers," see my book *Psychic Sight* to learn about the common angel numbers and their meanings. Everyone's guides will look different and they may have a similar

27

signature as mine or they may be different. I am not sure since I have only seen the signature of my one group.

My guides appear to me as three Caucasian males and one appears to be a Native American that is a shapeshifter. Six guides in total with my two cats being two of my guides that incarnated into the physical to assist me in this incarnation. The energetic signature they leave me with after visiting or after I visit them in the 5th dimension is a fish jumping in and out of water that fades over 20 seconds upon waking. For everyone else out there that eventually sees the signatures, I am not sure if you will see the same fish signature for your guides. If you see a signature other than mine, please contact me and let me know, I would love to know what you see for your guides also. I will now move on to some common 4th dimensional beings.

Spider

These beings are kind of hit or miss. They are either malicious or non-malicious. Based on how their signature looks, they appear to look like a small spider. When I have encountered these beings they usually minded their own business but they would stare. In dreams, they would appear as animals but they would have a distorted face, similar to how a person or animal who is afflicted with down syndrome might look and they would stare intently.

Mechanical Spider

Much different from the spider entity and much bigger. The signature of this being appeared to be a giant spider although it appeared mechanical in nature as if it were engineered. This is one of the most malevolent beings you can come into contact with, they are highly malicious. These beings can come to you as nightmares and will attach themselves to your spine and inflict a painful extraction process on you. When I have been attacked by these mechanical spiders I felt the pain while asleep, and waking up from the pain, I would still feel the pain resonating in that same spot for minutes, even hours after waking. Their piercing ability can leave holes in your energetic field, they have a powerful pinch.

Fairies

Similar to the spider entity, fairies are hit or miss and usually not malicious although the ones not of the highest good can be tricksters. These beings, based on their signature, look closely relatable to the fairy in the Peter Pan cartoon, Tinker Bell. If anything I would say the artwork for Tinker Bell came inspired by seeing these beings. I would say the majority of fairies are neutral creatures, but like in anything, you have good and bad beings. The tricksters will trick you with illusions. All of these astral beings seem to be able to possess the ability to enter into your dream state and create an illusion to distract you while on the outside of the dream extracting your energy.

Imps

These creatures usually flock together in a group, highly malicious. They appear to look like small winged creatures with a tail. They look fleshless, like skeletal birds. These bad boys can possess you in the dream state. When I encountered these, I had been woken up saying I was making a loud vibrating noise while asleep. In dreams they appeared in, I was trying to warn people of incoming dangers and they would possess me to prevent me from warning the public and would try to drown me.

Skeleton Figures

This group looks how you might envision the grim reaper to look. A skeleton with a shroud over the head. I am almost positive this is a conjured minion. I have seen them solo and in a group coming through a green portal. These creatures are instructed by a master to extract and obtain energy.

Succubus

One of the most common and world-renowned astral beings known throughout the world, the succubus. This malicious feminine astral being is known for its sexual seduction of men. People with an uncleansed pineal gland and unactivated third eye may see this female being appearing as a shadowy figure or a black fog.

When you are able to see this being, she looks like a beautiful female humanoid type of being however she has this energetic aura of straight-up pure negativity that radiates off of her very essence. Contrary to popular depictions of the succubus, they do not have horns or wings. Their skin is the color of black coal, extremely black. Their hair is long and smooth looking like silk.

As a male, if you have a "wet dream," you may be familiar with the term nocturnal emission. If you have a sexual dream, it is the work of an astral being creating an illusion of themselves as an attractive individual and extracting your sexual energy. Once you train yourself to become lucid, or aware, while dreaming and you deny the sexual advance in the dream, you will quickly find out that it is not just a dream as it is at this point they will drop the illusion and rape you instead since you are refusing to be consensual. As long as you are consensual to the sexual act, they will play nice and allow you to believe you are only dreaming. Succubus normally only visits males however, they can go for women also. They have the ability to keep you in the paralysis state and energetically rape a person.

Incubus

The incubus is the world-renown male version of the succubus. Since I am a male, I do not have much to offer on a description of this being since I have not encountered it enough times. I have had one visit me trying to quickly extract some sexual energy from me but I woke up and caught him and invoked my authority over him to leave my space. They are pretty similar to the succubus description above though. They can appear as shadowy figures in the room or a black fog during sleep paralysis. These beings mostly go after women but as my testimony implies, they can go for males also. These beings also have the ability to keep you in a paralysis state and energetically rape a person.

Hag

Similar to the succubus, the hag is old-looking feminine beings who are astral witches. They have the ability to shapeshift. I noticed her signature usually represents a bird-like creature. The Hag is harder to catch, she is very elusive and subtle. She is definitely patient, she will wait hours for you to fall asleep to swoop in. Hags prefer sexual acts to extract energy. Leaves scratch marks on the body after visiting that appear as physically scarred over lines across the body. These marks could look similar to as if a cat had scratched you and it healed over.

Energetic Ethereal Beings

There are many types of these kinds of beings and they all look different. They are transparent in nature, you can see them but they appear to be see-through. These beings can be neutral or malicious. The common ones are known as Djinn, or Genie. These are very powerful astral entities, as I mentioned some are negative some are neutral/positive. They can also be attached to objects in the physical such as crystals or an artifact. Contrary to popular beliefs, they do not grant you three wishes however they can make offers to you. I encountered a Djinn only because he was attached to a Atlantean Record Keeper Crystal I was given by someone completely at random. They said they felt led to give it to me. I did not discover it was a record keeper until six months later. When this Djinn appeared to me, he looked like a giant blue transparent/ethereal deity inside my wall while I astral projected.

There is biased information about them on the internet about this group of beings being negative entities. Understand there are both positive and negative beings in every race of beings including humans, it is not bound to an entire group of species. You have to discern the spirits. If they are not for your highest good, cast them aside. I have not had a negative experience with the Genies as I have only encountered one and he shared wisdom with me. I still advise caution with dealing with one of these beings if you encounter one. Entities cannot interact with you without your permission so if you do not want it, make it known with your authority and decline permission for visitations.

Chapter 4

Signs of Entity Presence

Since I can see entities and most people on average cannot quite yet see them in the physical, I will try to explain and describe scenarios to help you identify when one is present in your life. Obviously sleep paralysis is the title of this book so it would be one of the biggest indicators.

However, sleep paralysis is also linked to astral projecting, or consciously leaving the body and traveling. So you have to do a little process of elimination. Keep a dream journal so you can jot down all your experiences and so that it will help you remember those experiences such as what happened in the dream or paralysis state and what you saw and felt. Dreaming is our imagination at work. One of the biggest indicators that your dream is more than a dream is that you will have access to all your five senses. In normal dreams you will not feel anything, taste anything, or smell anything, only see and hear.

If you are finding yourself overly fatigued after sleeping for hours there may be energy extraction at play. Something unique about me is I can function with a few hours of sleep and no caffeine. I wake up every 2 hours and I do not use an alarm clock to get up for work since I wake up so often. This is an everyday reality for me and I have plenty of energy in the mornings and do not drink caffeine nor am I tired or fatigued. If you are overly tired after having 7-8 hours or so of rest, then that is an indicator that you are tired because there's a lack of energy there so that is another thing to be wary of.

The easiest sign that is a no brainer is sexual dreams. You might think that it is just a dream, try becoming lucid while that dream is taking place and deny the sexual advance, see what happens. Whether the entity that is having sex with you is a negative or positive being, you'll have to discern that for yourself. Not everyone has sexual dreams either and it is mostly men since we can struggle to control lustful urges during younger years but get a grip on it as we get older. With that being said there are tons of female beings out there getting plenty of energy from men via siphoning through sexual dreams because men on average will naturally be consensual to it. One of the biggest lessons for a soul incarnating into a male body is overcoming sexual lust. Now I am not saying sex is bad at all or having a ton of it with your partner is bad. I am saying when it is all you think about and if you are not getting it as much as you want so your cheating on your partner, swiping on Tinder while in a relationship, overly seeking women for sexual purposes, etc., then you are ruled by it and one of your lessons is to overcome it.

Feeling pain in your dreams is also a red flag. If you feel pain and it feels real, there could be some foul play there, especially if you feel it anywhere along the spine. Keep in mind the big indicator that having access to your five senses while dreaming is not a dream. It could be a message, a past life memory recollection, someone trying to communicate with you, and sure of course or an entity, etc.. Also note that if your partner is saying you are making weird noises in your sleep, and not just sleep talking, but actual crazy noises that you would not be able to replicate while awake.

Chapter 5

Energetic Marking/Implants

As I mentioned briefly in a previous chapter, once a negative entity encounters you or you encounter it, they can place an energetic mark/implant on you. These implants can remain on you for life. These implants help the entity stay connected to you. In order for negative entities to extract our energy, they have to pierce our auric field. This piercing effect also leaves a hole behind, allowing entry into it. With that being said, there are entities that are parasitic and they can attach themselves inside your auric field by entering in through one of these holes.

Entities can influence us when they are connected with us. A person might have life long addictions that they feel they cannot get rid of.

A person might have a high sexual addiction, drug

addiction, substance addiction, etc.. These hard to break-free-from addictions come from an energetic parasite living within your energetic body. One might find it difficult to break an addiction because they have an energetic bond with an entity they are unaware of. For high sexual addictions, there is most likely a parasite living in your sacral chakra which is connected to sexuality and creativity. Energy healing practitioners, such as Reiki Masters, can scan for and remove these implants, remove the parasites, and repair the holes within the auric field. If these addictions are habits one has tried to break before but could not, they may find that once the parasite is removed that the addiction is suddenly gone.

A low vibration also allows entities to enter into our auric field (See **Vibration** in **Chapter 6** to learn what this is). If a person hurts one emotionally and one becomes sad, depressed, or angry, an entity can take advantage of this and come to try to attach themselves to this person and form a bond. When a person is under the influence of a substance or alcohol this allows negative entities that have a bond with the person greater influence over the body. They can somewhat take over and influence you to do things you otherwise would not while sober. Ever wonder why they call wine spirits? We on average consciously believe we are making conscious decisions to make negative choices when we make negative decisions. Positive beings can also provide this same effect that may come in a form of intuition to persuade you away from a situation or scenario that is not for your highest good or may end up harming you. That is, of course, if you listen.

When we are aware we can be greatly influenced by unseen beings, it brings awareness to the fact that negative/intuitive thoughts you might be having are not your own thoughts but are beings trying to influence you for negative/positive reasons. Lower vibrational emotions fuel negative beings. Emotions such as fear, anger, and depression. In rare severe cases, entities can completely take over your body and possess you. This would only happen with your permission of course and you might not have any recollection of what happened during the possession.

If you meet an extremely negative person that is toxic

to everyone they come into contact with, they without a doubt have formed a bond with a negative entity they may or may not know of. It is important to stay away from negative people, even family members, that show continuous negative behavior. The entities involved in their life can also come on to you and start affecting your life. Sleeping in the same house as this person will affect everyone living in the house. Until the person with the bond attached denounces and has the removal of this bond, the entity can mess with any person that comes into contact with this bonded individual if you stick around them a little too long.

I do not have a history of nightmares but I can share that when I have slept at homes with an extremely toxic individual living there, I would continuously have nightmares at night. The dark does not like the light. As long as you remain positive, full of love for others, full of light, you cannot be influenced by negative entities, period. Positivity and love are the highest levels of vibration. Fear, anger, negativity, and toxicity, are all examples of the lowest levels of vibration. Entities can only affect those remaining in a lower vibrational state.

Raise yourself by healing traumas in your life, forgiving others that have wronged you (forgiving does not mean you have to communicate or allow them back into your life), shifting negative mindsets, surrounding yourself around positive like-minded people, and eating organic plant-based foods. As long as you operate in the love frequency, you are impenetrable.

Chapter 6

How to Protect Yourself

In this chapter, I will explain what you can do to protect yourself against entities. Having been attacked by these beings throughout my life, I know what works and what does not work. In my desperation, I tried most things that there is currently information about in modern days.

What I can tell you is that there is no better defense than setting up a crystal grid. I will be the first to admit that I did not even believe it would work. This is before I had any knowledge about crystals. I thought there was no way four little crystals I spent a dollar apiece on would prevent attacks I had been suffering from for years. Allow me to tell you about the supernatural defensive barrier of a Clear Quartz grid.

Clear Quartz Grid

A Clear Quartz Crystal is a commonly known crystal that is renowned for its protective properties similar to that of the black crystal named Tourmaline. When you form a grid in your room with these crystals, it forms an invisible barrier that acts as a filter to prevent negative energetic entry.

If you live in an apartment you can barrier each room or just your main room you sleep in. If you live in a house you can barrier the outdoors of the house placing a crystal at each corner or wall to wall. To create this barrier, (you can burn some sage and let it cleanse the crystals first if you want but it is not necessary since Clear Quartz is a natural protective crystal) first figure out how many crystals you need.

You will need two per wall to wall corner. For a room, rooms are usually square or four-sided, you would only need four crystals however some rooms have weird angles so that is why I say two per wall to wall. If you do not believe in talking to the crystals you do not have to do this part but I believe intent strengthens the purpose of what you want the crystal to specifically do but like I mentioned when I first did it for myself I did not even believe it would work. I just placed them and waited to see if it did anything and it still worked. Hold the crystals in your hand with the left hand. If you want to imbue it with energies to give it some more strength imagine blue energy emitting from the left hand into the crystals, and cover them with the right hand.

Again if you want to imbue some energies into it, imagine a violet flame energy emitting from the right hand into the crystals. Tell the crystals out loud or in your mind what you want them to do specifically and then thank them for their protection. Then place one crystal at every corner so that it forms a barrier that the human eyes cannot see. Remember wall to wall, so for a room that is square, you would place four crystals. If it has weird angles place them at each corner. If you have small animals that might tamper with them you may need to tape the crystals to the wall.

Once placed, the first night you sleep within the barrier you may experience waking up once an hour or odd times. Not everyone experiences this but most people including myself experienced this or other subtle abnormalities during the first night. Do not worry, this only happens the first night. I do not know why this happens but I understand it is some type of integration. I will go over some other things that also help however this is by far the best defense against entities and you will not find this information online because it is not a known technique. That is why it was a part of my experience and journey to obtain this information and provide it to as many as I can.

Sage

Sage is a herb. Dried sage, most commonly known as white sage, has traditionally been used by Native Americans as a method for purification. You can take dry sage, burn it, and use it to purify the negative energies inside an object or the space that you dwell in. Now do not get it twisted, sage does not protect you against entities, it can ward them off but once it is done burning and cleared they can come right back. I burned a mountain of sage before sleep, even let it go while sleeping and they kept coming, right after in fact. Understand sage only clears the object or environment within that moment in time. Once the sage dissipates, negative entities can come back. That is why crystal gridding is the best form of defense since it offers 24/7 protection.

Cats

Get yourself a cat. You could say dogs are protectors of the physical realm and cats are protectors of the spiritual realm. Cats sleep ⅔ of their life. They are connected to the astral realms more than we realize. They are very much playful animals in the physical, but their higher selves are guardians in the astral realms. Cats were revered in ancient Egyptian times. In fact, it was punishable by law so that if you harmed a cat you would be sentenced to death.

Cats can go to battle for us because they have a natural instinct to protect the people they are bonded with out of love. This could result in them becoming sick or obtaining an illness. They can intervene and take a blow for their owners against spiritual attacks. Oftentimes cats choose the family they are going to protect against spiritual attacks prior to incarnating. We believe we choose the cat, the truth is they come into our lives at the correct time they are needed. Contrary to popular belief, cats have more than nine lives. They can incarnate as many times as they want to. A kitten could incarnate at a specific time just to help a family against an entity, get sick as a result from the astral battle, and die for that family in the physical but move on to the next phase of existence or mission. Purposely knowing that they would die but do it nonetheless anyways out of pure unconditional love. This particular animal soul could possibly reincarnate right after that to continue to be with that specific family as another cat.

Maintaining a High Vibration

What is vibration? Our reality is made up of energy, frequencies, and vibrations. All matter is made up of atoms which is energy that is constantly vibrating. Solid objects appear to be still but are actually vibrating at a speed so fast that we perceive objects as being still. Understand that vibration is energy and energy is vibration. As humans, we are pure energy.

The state of your vibration can be figured out by your state of being. One either vibrates at a low frequency, low to middle frequency, middle frequency, middle to high frequency, or a high frequency, etc.. Energy is also affected by frequencies. Humans are energy therefore we are affected by frequencies. Look at Wi-Fi for example.

Wi-Fi is a frequency that we cannot see however our devices are able to pick up on this frequency and allow our technological devices to connect to the internet. Same with radios and antennas. We are constantly surrounded by different vibrational frequencies. Frequencies can also harm us, animals, and insects. I am sure you have seen commercials for the device (Ultrasonic Pest Repellers) that repels rodents and insects that plugs into the wall in a home.

It does this by emitting electromagnetic frequency waves. The U.S. military has also used 5G frequency wave technology to disperse crowds from a distance and disorient people in an area. In fact, long exposure to 5G frequencies has been proven to cause flu-like symptoms, severe vomiting, and death. So with this understanding, it is evident that vibrations and frequencies play a major role within our reality.

Think of vibrating at a high frequency as a barrier.

The higher you are vibrating, the stronger and more impenetrable your barrier is. The lower you vibrate, the weaker and more fragile your barrier is. Negative entities are low vibrational beings so they can only affect those with a non-high vibration. Once a person's vibration is too high, entities cannot penetrate your energetic field to extract your energy.

Maintaining a low vibration also affects your immune system. The lower your vibration, the more susceptible you are to catching a sickness or illness. The higher it is the less likely you are to become sick and you will fight off sicknesses more quickly. Those with a low vibration are often fearful, quick to anger, negative about themselves or others, depressed, have a disregard for others, lack of love for others, etc.

These negative emotions weaken, or lower, your vibration. Those with a high vibration are full of positivity, unconditional love for others, peaceful, and full of compassion. To raise your vibration from a low vibration to a higher vibration, you have to change your mentality and become the ruler of your emotions and not ruled by them. Understand that there is nothing to fear in this reality. We are all a part of a great cosmic plan and we each have our own unique individual journey and gifts to contribute to the world. Let go of anger, walk in love, forgive others, love others, and help others while expecting nothing back in return. Good deeds are not overlooked and are returned back to you x3 in karma. Karma is timeless. It could be repaid to you tomorrow, a year from now, 5 years, 10 years, or in the next incarnation. There is no escape from karma whether positive or negative. Eat high vibrational foods such as organic fruits, vegetables, and plant-based foods and nutrients. Animal meat from our market-places is a low vibrational substance since it contains the energies of physical trauma, torture, death, fear, etc.. Consuming meat, dairy, and animal bi-products will keep your vibration lower than it could be. Yes, even dairy as milk from cows is obtained through a means of torture. Cows are only able to produce milk up to a year after birthing a calf. Cows are forced into pregnancy and are constantly having their milk extracted (the same thing entities do to humans via energy siphon) for usually up to 3 years then they are culled (killed). With this understanding, you may now have an understanding of why most of the population is lactose intolerant. The human body does not want to occupy negative energy. I am not saying you need to change your diet, I am only informing you on how to raise your vibration and this is one of the ways. Do what works best for you. Do your research, there are a wide variety of alternatives and are easily accessible in today's age.

Chapter 7

Telepathy and Reprogramming
the Subconscious

You might have caught me a few times in previous chapters mentioning invoking my authority over an entity. Things seem to be based on agreements outside of our physical realm. I have come to learn that there are cosmic laws that beings have to abide by.

One of the laws is that a being cannot have continuous interactions with another being without consent and this is based on my experience so I am not 100% sure if this is a real law. If a being visits you, you seemingly have authority over them to tell them to leave but you have to recognize your own authority and be specific when communicating. There are loopholes these negative beings will utilize and they are professional loophole finders like lawyers. You may quickly realize that when trying to speak to an entity during sleep paralysis, your mouth is bound and you can only mumble so you cannot issue out your authority. Communication is not spoken through the mouth outside of the physical realm, it is spoken with the mind, telepathy. You have to train yourself to speak with the mind and not always the mouth. Through a great inner web, we are all connected. So to speak via telepathy is not impossible, it is a very real thing. The tricky part is on average we are ignorant of this fact and are often too ignorant to acknowledge or be aware of our authority over them. The Bible also talks about this authority over beings not in the physical.

As I mentioned, things seem to be very contractual outside of our realm. I am sure you have heard of people signing over their soul for riches in the physical, it is an agreement you have to consent to. So like these visitations, there has to be an agreement or consent. One loophole is by not saying yes or no to these visitations, it is considered the same as allowing consent for them to continue visiting and extracting your energy. You have to specifically tell them, no, leave now, you do not have my permission to be here, respect cosmic law and leave my space and never return, through telepathy. They do not understand English so if you do not reciprocate proper communication, again, it is the same as allowing consent for them to keep visiting and extracting your energy as a loophole. When you speak through telepathy your message is interpreted into their mind as their language.

Likewise, when we receive telepathy we will hear it as the language we are most familiar with. Again, you have to have conviction when you speak to these beings, recognize your authority over them, you do not have to submit to them, they have to submit to you. Let go of fear, be fearless, fear nothing. Negative beings are of the lowest vibration, they have no power over you, they can only take advantage of ignorance, much like our government and media. The only control they have on us is the control we allow them to have. There seems to be a type of law that whatever question you ask a being, they by law have to answer. If you are concerned about the intent of an entity visitation, you can question them by asking them are you a being of the highest good, are you for my highest good, are your intentions for my highest good, etc.. They have to answer and sly ones will try to indirectly answer or try to be deceitful in the response by indirectly answering. You need to be able to discern and read between the lines to see if there is any deceit in their response. A being for your highest good will express no deceit period.

You can learn to reprogram your subconscious to do a task. The human body is the greatest computer on Earth. There is no computer that can do what the human body can do. You can issue commands to your body right before falling asleep and this will reprogram your subconscious. Our conscious mind reacts to the beliefs of the subconscious. These commands can also carry over while dreaming. Some example of commands:

I remember my dreams, I am fearless, I am not afraid of water, I am not afraid of fire, I am not afraid of thunderstorms, I am not afraid of astral beings, I am not afraid of spiders, I am not afraid of snakes, I am beautiful, I am powerful, I am abundant, I am protected, I am guided by divine beings, I become lucid while dreaming, I will become aware when I dream, I will not allow entities/astral beings to extract my energy, I do not consent to sexual dreams, my energy is my own, I do not share my energy.

Literally any command you wish to issue to your subconscious you just get into a routine of repeating it to yourself in your mind prior to falling asleep IN PRESENT TENSE VERBIAGE ONLY. This will reprogram your subconscious to make it a conscious belief.

The subconscious only understands present tense, do not use past or future tense words. Whatever you consciously believe is bridged into your reality through the law of attraction. So be careful if you issue negative commands about yourself and repeat daily such as, *I am ugly, I am not smart, I am stupid, it's my fault, I am useless, I hate myself, no one loves me, I am alone, I am not worthy, I am not beautiful, bad things always happen to me, my relationships never work out, I hate life, I hate living,* it becomes a programmed conscious belief in your subconscious and the universe will keep this belief as apart of your reality to match your vibrational frequency. So yes, you will continue to live in a reality that is harmonious with your ritualistic beliefs. The universe is neutral, all it sees is neutrality, so it will bridge into your reality your conscious beliefs and your beliefs are the things you repeat to yourself every day and wholeheartedly believe. The law of attraction is neutral, it works for positive beliefs and negative beliefs. Stay positive and self heal the traumas placed in your life by yourself and others. Heal the genetic curses that have carried through your family lineage. Tell yourself, it stops here with me. Be the resolution, be that outcast, be that difference, be that trendsetter, be that 1 in 1000. The outcasts of the family are typically the geniuses anyways, food for thought.

Conclusion

In conclusion, I hope this book will have helped bring some clarity to those who have been afflicted with sleep paralysis or seeing figures at night and having no understanding about it or why it is happening. I am glad to have shared information that will help you identify unseen beings that co-exist with us within our reality and helpful methods/techniques you can use to protect yourself.

There is something I would like you to take from this book. Everything that happens in your life serves a divine purpose. Every person you encounter serves a contractual purpose. Every being you encounter serves a cosmic purpose. Without negative, there would be no understanding of positive. Without positive, there would be no understanding of negative. Going forward in your life, understand that there is no good or bad, there is only neutrality, the yin and yang, the balance.

The reason opposites exist is so that we have an understanding of both perspectives. These negative beings are allowed to be involved in our life for growth. That is why I have always appreciated them, the negative and the positive beings. Without their many lessons, I could not provide the information I am providing you now. Our souls want to grow and evolve. We can forget that after incarnating here and get lost in the grand scheme of living in the physical in these modern times. Everything is so fast-paced, we have to work long hours, we have families to take care of, we lack the time to appreciate the moment, etc.

We forget that our souls came here for development, for growth, to help the Earth, to help humanity, to aid all of creation. These entities play a part in forcing us to grow through negative experiences to force us into our true light because we get comfortable and like to remain still. Their part of the plan is to create problems, our part is to acknowledge and fix those problems within ourselves first because we have to first fix ourselves before we can help others. Some overcome the obstacles these entities bring with ease, some are a little bit more challenged by these obstacles, and some never overcome their obstacles and will have to try again in the next incarnation. That is the purpose. The soul demands growth, it does not care how you feel about growth, the material things you possess, how known you are, how poor you are, how rich you are. The soul has one main priority and that is evolution. Evolution is inevitable. Until we decide to grow from experience to experience, our realities are presented with the same issue over and over in a continuous loop until we have overcome it. We then move on to the next obstacle our soul wants to experience growth in, it is a never-ending cycle of consistent growth and evolution.

There is nothing to fear from these entities as they have a part to play in the great plan of the cosmos just as we do. People and beings sometimes come into our lives temporarily so that we can encounter an experience with them and grow from it. The good or bad aspect of it is solely based on individual perspective.

A negative experience could lead to a positive outcome in the long term or to prepare you for something in the future. An example is how could you appreciate a good relationship if you never had a bad relationship. Maybe you would need to experience several bad relationships to prepare you for your soul mate in the future. If you did not have the proper growth prior to meeting your soulmate connection, it would not work so you have to be conditioned in order for your paths to align otherwise the universe keeps you separated until you both equally vibrate at the same frequency. Accept these temporary interactions for growth and then when the time comes to let them go, let them go and continue forward.

Through a great inner web we are all connected as one of the many great lines stated in Disney's classic animated movie, Pocahontas, stated, "we are all connected to each other, in a circle, in a hoop, that never ends" (Pocahontas soundtrack, *Colors of the Wind*, *1995*). And if you have not heard this song I encourage you to listen to it. In 3 minutes and 34 seconds, you will learn the basic fundamentals of everything you need to know about how all beings are connected and by raising our individual awareness first, our own mentality and selves are healed.

That inevitably raises global awareness, improves global mentality, and shifts collective consciousness towards the love frequency. Since we are all connected, healing ourselves... globally heals everyone collectively. We are all apart of a mass consciousness. Embrace the balance, walk in love and neutrality my brothers and sisters. Peace, love, and abundance is upon you.

About the Author

Johnny is a 29-year-old Creek Native American from Tulsa, Oklahoma. He currently lives in Conway, Arkansas providing spiritual and metaphysical services for his local community. Since a young age, Johnny has been able to see things within our reality that are naturally invisible to us. He has been able to see and speak with spirits and entities throughout his life.

Initially, he believed being plagued with this connection as being able to have these abilities made it challenging to function in a society such as how we live in today's age that does not recognize on a global scale that beings other than humans exist. Having no one to share this information without being accused of being crazy or having a medical disorder, he tuned them out earlier in his life until the visits became less frequent and began to cease. Even though he had toned them out, the spirits still aided him from behind the scenes, guiding and teaching him along the way. When he became older, he started to return back to his spiritual roots and the spirits reappeared as if they had never left but only had remained hidden from view.

Johnny believes, as he has been led to believe by his spiritual council outside of our physical dimension, that he was a Native American shaman in a past life and he has been called again to continue his work in this life by providing healing, spiritual services, protection, and revelation about the unseen forces that exist within our reality to his community and citizens that he comes into contact with. Johnny can provide some services from a distance via phone or webcam.

He mentions that with permission from the client he can provide a few of his services to clients anywhere in the world as their permission allows him to connect to their energy and the spirits that preside over them. Johnny extends an invitation to connect with him regarding any questions or concerns you might have related to spiritual matters or about his books. Contact him on Facebook or Instagram, links provided.

www.Facebook.com/Johnny52020

www.Instagram.com/J5_2020

CPSIA information can be obtained
at www.ICGtesting.com
Printed in the USA
BVHW061620070920
588240BV00013B/1678

9 781578 432066